WHEN DINOSAURS LIVED
Velociraptor
KATE RIGGS

Published by
CREATIVE PAPERBACKS

P.O. Box 227, Mankato, Minnesota 56002
Creative Paperbacks is an imprint of The Creative Company
www.thecreativecompany.us

Design and production by Danny Nanos of Gilbert & Nanos
Art direction by Rita Marshall
Printed in the United States of America

Photographs by Corbis (Louie Psihoyos, Louie Psihoyos/Science Faction),
Getty Images (DEA Picture Library, Dorling Kindersley, Yoshikazu Tsuno/AFP),
Library of Congress, Photolibrary (Oxford Scientific)

The Library of Congress has cataloged the hardcover edition as follows:
Riggs, Kate.
Velociraptor / by Kate Riggs.
p. cm. — (When dinosaurs lived)
Summary: A brief introduction to the speedy *Velociraptor*,
highlighting its size, habitat, food sources, and demise. Also included is a
virtual field trip to a museum with notable *Velociraptor* fossils.

Includes bibliographical references and index.

ISBN 978-1-60818-121-6 (hardcover)
ISBN 978-1-62832-213-2 (Developmental Studies Center edition)

1. Velociraptor—Juvenile literature. I. Title. II. Series: When dinosaurs lived.

QE862.S3R5525 2015

567.912—dc23   2014048594

This edition published specially for Developmental Studies
Center 2015 by The Creative Company.

2 4 6 8 9 7 5 3 1

Table of Contents

Velociraptor was a theropod dinosaur. It lived from 75 to 70 million years ago. The name *Velociraptor* means "swift thief."

Some people think *Velociraptor* had spots or stripes on its skin

Velociraptor: *veh-LAH-si-RAP-tor*

Velociraptor was a fast-running meat-eater. It had about 80 sharp teeth, and it was always ready to eat prey. It had large eyes on the sides of its head, like a bird. This helped *Velociraptor* see all around.

Velociraptor ran on two legs and ate prey of all sizes

An adult *Velociraptor* weighed only about 33 pounds (15 kg). It stood three to four feet (0.9–1.2 m) tall. *Velociraptor* used speed to make up for its small size. The **predator** chased its larger prey at speeds of up to 40 miles (64 km) per hour.

Two huge claws on the back feet were sharp weapons

Velociraptor lived in dry deserts. There was not much water in the deserts. *Velociraptor* stayed on the move during the day. It ran quickly over the hot sand with its four-toed feet.

The place where *Velociraptor* lived is now called the Gobi Desert

The small, horned dinosaur *Protoceratops* was one of *Velociraptor's* favorite meals. *Protoceratops* was a plant-eater, but *Velociraptor* also hunted other meat-eaters. It ate fast-running meat-eaters such as *Oviraptor* and *Gallimimus*.

Velociraptor sometimes fought each other over food

Velociraptor spent most of the time looking for food. Sometimes *Velociraptor* traveled in packs, or groups. *Velociraptor* died out about 70 million years ago. Five million years later, all the dinosaurs disappeared.

Velociraptor packs attacked larger prey like *Saurolophus*

Scientists know about *Velociraptor* because they have studied fossils. Fossils are the remains of living things that died long ago. Many fossils of *Velociraptor* have been found on the **continent** of Asia. The first one was found in 1923.

Fossils of *Velociraptor* relatives called dromaeosaurids have also been found

Velociraptor compared with a five-foot-tall (152 cm) person

Paleontologists are people who study dinosaurs. Henry Fairfield Osborn was the paleontologist who named *Velociraptor*. He called it "swift thief" because he thought it stole other dinosaurs' eggs for food.

People used to think that *Velociraptor* was like a lizard and dragged its tail on the ground. Now people think that it was covered with fuzz or feathers and was more like a bird that does not fly. But scientists still study fossils of *Velociraptor*. There are more things to learn about this "swift thief"!

People in Japan made a model of *Velociraptor* with fur in 2008

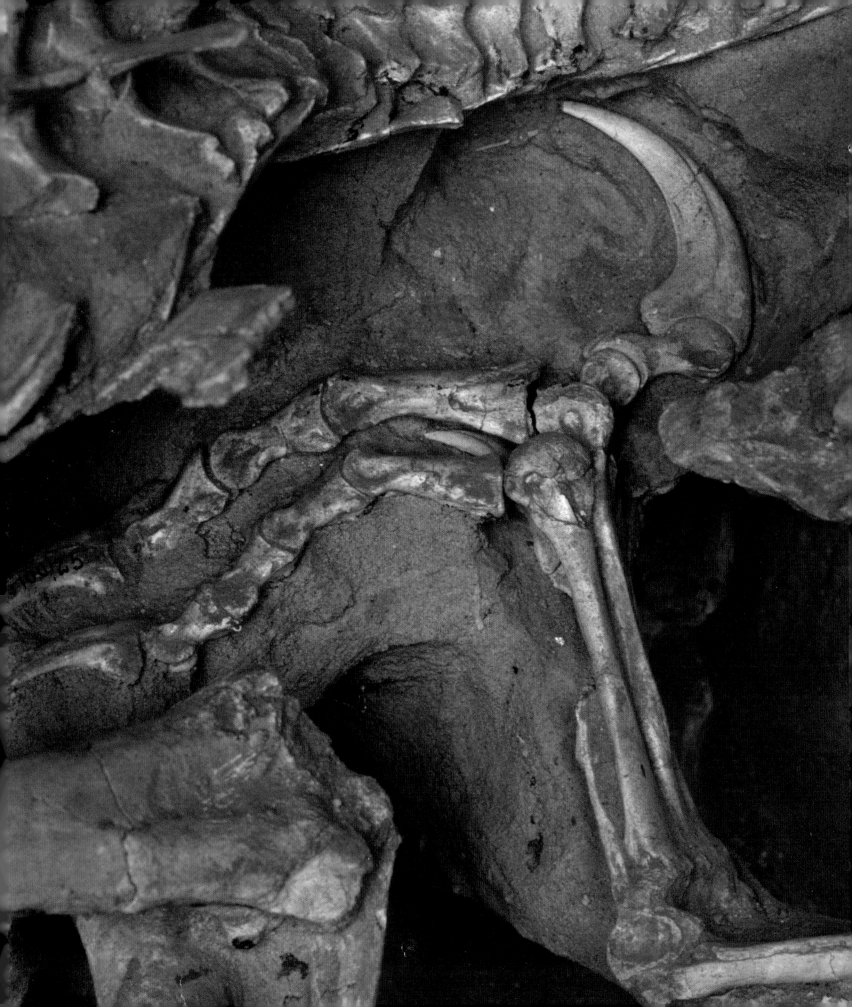

A Virtual Field Trip: Museum of Natural History, Ulaanbaatar, Mongolia

You can see *Velociraptor* fighting *Protoceratops* in Mongolia's Museum of Natural History. The famous fossil is called "Fighting Dinosaurs" and was found in 1971. It was buried in the Gobi Desert of Mongolia, a country in eastern Asia. It shows *Velociraptor* with a claw in *Protoceratops*'s throat. The dinosaurs were probably fighting in a sandstorm when they died like that.

Glossary

continent—one of Earth's seven big pieces of land
predators—animals that kill and eat other animals
prey—animals that are killed and eaten by other animals
theropod—a meat-eating dinosaur that walked on two legs

A close-up picture of the "Fighting Dinosaurs" fossil

Read More

Dixon, Dougal. *Meat-eating Dinosaurs*.
Mankato, Minn.: NewForest Press, 2011.

Johnson, Jinny. *Velociraptor and Other Speedy Killers*.
North Mankato, Minn.: Smart Apple Media, 2008.

Websites

Enchanted Learning: Velociraptor

http://www.enchantedlearning.com/subjects/dinosaurs/dinos/Velociraptor.shtml

This site has *Velociraptor* facts and a picture to color.

Velociraptor Coloring Page

http://www.first-school.ws/t/cpvelociraptor.htm

This site has a picture of *Velociraptor* that can be printed out and colored.